Special thanks to my parents who always love, encourage and support me. I couldn't have done this without them.

— Arianna M. Fox

Printed and Published by IngramSpark

One Ingram Blvd., La Vergne, TN 37086

Copyright © 2017 | Splash Designworks, LLC

All rights reserved. No part of this book may be reproduced or transmitted in any form by any means, electronic or mechanical, including photocopying, recording or by any information storage and retrieval systems without the written permission of Splash Designworks, LLC, except where permitted by law.

Book Illustrations by Annabell Bailor
Illustration edited by Mike Fox | Splash Designworks
Layout & Design by Mike Fox | Splash Designworks
Editing by Mike & Trisha Fox

For information or inquiries, please contact
SPLASH DESIGNWORKS
www.splashdw.com
info@splashdw.com

To book or schedule Arianna for your event, please contact
afox@bigideaskidcoaching.com
Visit online: www.bigideaskidcoaching.com

ISBN-10:
0-692-87695-2
ISBN-13:
978-0-692-87695-4

The story starts with Princess Brooke. She's very polite, tenderhearted and happy. But most of all, she's helpful.

along with four princesses who were also her best friends!

Laquita

Marina

Spring

Lenora

Brooke and her friends were outside having fun in a garden when the queen announced...

"Everyone, everyone! We're going to have a Wonderful Event! It will be called The Great Kingdom Event!"

Everyone was so excited, they were jumping, cheering and clapping! The queen announced that Princess Brooke will be setting the event up and that the other princesses will be helping with other things according to their talents!

"Let's all get to work!" the queen said.

Brooke was so excited about being the event leader that she forgot everyone was supposed to work together.

So Brooke went to visit Spring who was cleaning the swimming pool to get it ready for the event.

"Hey, Spring! How's it going?" Brooke asked.
"Hey, Brooke. Going great." replied Spring.

Then Brooke asked Spring, "Can I clean the pool for you?

I love to help!

After all, what are friends for, right?"

"Sure, Brooke! Thanks!" Spring replied with a smile.

Spring was thankful for Brooke wanting to help, but she really wanted to clean the pool herself.

Nevertheless, she let Brooke clean the pool for her.

Then Brooke was on her way to clean.

But when Brooke started cleaning the pool, she looked at the water and got distracted by her own reflection...

...and she accidentally spilled some of the pool cleaner on her beautiful dress.

And it made a huge stain!

Brooke passed by a mirror and saw the big stain on her dress in the reflection. So she thought about what else she could wear.

But Brooke got so distracted by deciding what to wear, she forgot that she told Spring she would clean the pool for her.

Being her friendly self, Brooke wanted to check on the rest of the princesses. So she went to visit Lenora who was practicing juggling for the event!

"How's it going, Lenora?" Brooke asked.

"Wonderful!" Lenora said while trying to concentrate.

"Can I do the juggling for you? I'm really good at it!" Brooke asked.

"Um, sure." Lenora replied, a little confused.

Lenora was thankful Brooke wanted to help, but since the queen gave her the job, she wanted to do it herself.

Nevertheless, she let Brooke juggle for her.

So Brooke was juggling for Lenora when she accidentally dropped the balls into the mud and they got all dirty.

She went to get some help to clean the juggling balls but she forgot that she already told Spring she would clean the pool.

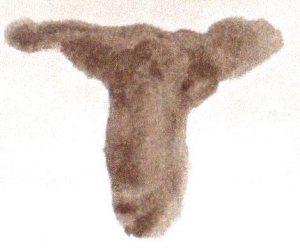

Then Brooke got distracted again and decided to visit Laquita, who was writing the invitations for the great event.

"Hey, Laquita!" Brooke said. "How's it going?"

"Great, Brooke! Just working on the invitations."

"Can I do those for you? I love to help!" Brooke asked.

"Um, sure, Brooke."
Laquita was thankful Brooke wanted to help, but she was excited to create the invitations herself.

Nevertheless, she let Brooke create the invitations for her.

Then Brooke looked up at the clock and saw that the event would be starting soon! But since she had taken all the jobs on herself, she didn't have time to complete any of them.

Brooke was just about to tell the queen what happened when suddenly a bell rang!

The queen announced, "Everyone has 20 minutes to finish their tasks, and then the Great Kingdom event will begin!"

Knowing that the tasks were not completed, Brooke asked the queen if she could postpone the event.

The wise queen said, "Brooke. You gave me your word that you would get these tasks completed in time, and we've already made the announcement. Sorry, I can't change it now."

Brooke ran to the other princesses to apologize. "I'm so sorry I didn't keep my word and tried to do everything myself."

"We forgive you," said the princesses.
"That's what friends are for, Brooke!" Laquita said with a smile.

Then the princesses rushed to finish their tasks just in time for the Great Kingdom event which turned out to be a huge success!

"Hmmm," Brooke said to herself. "It's because of teamwork!" she said with a smile.

Princess Brooke wants us to remember to always keep our word. We should want to help, but everyone has their own talents and gifts to use for the kingdom. Also, remember that together we can make anything happen if we use teamwork, because we can't do everything by ourselves. And if you make a mistake, just say you're sorry and ask for forgiveness. Hey, that's what friends are for, right?

Arianna is 100% family girl! She is the Jr. Marketing Director for her parents' (Mike & Trisha Fox) company Splash Designworks, which is an award winning creative ad, design, branding and digital marketing agency. (www.splashdw.com)

Her hobbies include a lot of writing, making electronic music with her own music name of JamTrax, helping her daddy with design and even his EDM music (Dubblestep).

Arianna enjoys extreme thrill rides, outside fun, rollerblading, dancing, having fun on her iPad and even doing Voice-over acting work!

Her parents, Mike & Trisha Fox also conduct lots of workshops both for their business and marriage coaching where Arianna has spoken many times.

Arianna has spoken at the 1 Million Cups Entrepreneurship Program, and has been featured in many news media outlets for her inspirational speaking. Her own website is at www.bigideaskidcoaching.com and she loves to leave her audiences with the mantra, *"You Rock! Dream Big, and You've Got This!"*

"When it comes to talent and professionalism, Arianna is light years ahead of your average Tween. Her ability to confidently give presentations in front of other professionals is second to none."

- ARIC CARNEY, *Regional Sales Manager, SOLAR CITY*

www.**bigideaskidcoaching**.com

- **KIDPRENEUR**
- **INSPIRATIONAL SPEAKING**
- **KID & YOUTH MENTORING**
- **KID COACHING**

FOR BOOKING
302.399.7851
afox@bigideaskidcoaching.com

Featured

DELAWARE NEWS JOURNAL

MILFORDLIVE MEDIA

FOX21 / WBOC TV

DISNEY'S BABBLE

www.ingramcontent.com/pod-product-compliance
Lightning Source LLC
Chambersburg PA
CBHW061817290426
44110CB00026B/2895